Swimming Lessons on the Titanic

Paul Richmond

Published by Human Error Publishing
www.humanerrorpublishing.com
paul@humanerrorpublishing.com

Copyright © 2022
by
Human Error Publishing & Paul Richmond

All Rights Reserved

ISBN: 978-1-948521-10-9

Cover design
Paul Richmond

Cover photo: Eva Schachtl

Bio photo Irina Smychkovich

Human Error Publishing asks that no part of this publication be reproduced or transmitted in any form or by any means electronic or mechanical, including photocopy, recording or information storage or retrieval system without permission in writing from Paul Richmond and Human Error Publishing. The reasons for this are to help support the publisher and the artists.

Dedicated to

Those who have read my work

Where to start

There's always a beginning

Hello

An introduction
Is this going to be casual
Or will this be heart wrenching

He said he felt old
For new beginnings
Yet isn't every day
Each breath
A new beginning

Where is the story going?
Are we in the middle?
Or nearing the end?
It depends
On whose story
We are talking about
Who is the Main Character?

My name is Paul Richmond

Here's Where They Live

I Need A Pen	10
Bus Ticket	11
Are You Ready For A Change	14
Billy Deserved It	18
Clouds, Hopes, Dreams	20
Don't Forget the Merch	22
The Door	24
Family Traditions	26
Firing Squad	28
Grocery Bagger at 70	31
Change Direction	34
Flash Cards	37
Merry Christmas 1970's	40
The Time I Met Hunter Thompson	44
I Think He Could've Made It	47
In The Streets	48
It's Not Working	50

Here's Where They Live

Leaving Soon	53
Looking Out the Window	54
Lost...............Released	56
She Told Me - She Was the Devil's Mistress	60
Mommy Why	62
My New Year's resolution - 2021	63
Patron Saint of Lost Causes	64
Pissing in the Front Yard	66
Who Works for Who	69
Wrong Person	72
You'er A White Man	74
Grandpa was a Sonofabitch	78
I Hate This Place	79
What Do You Do For A Living	80
Amazed	83
The School for the Protection of the Arts	84
The King of the Killers	86
Culture	89
Bug Splat	92
Who Are You	96

I Need A Pen

I went to the bank
I don't have any money
To put in the bank
But they have free pens

After awhile
They notice
Every time I come in
The pens need to be restocked

Some banks have put chains on their pens
So I have to
Keep finding new banks

I suppose it would be easier
If I didn't lose the pens

Bus Ticket

Sir
Do you have your bus ticket

I thought I had it right here
(searching pockets)

Sir you will need a bus ticket
If you want to get on this bus

I had it just a minute ago

That's an old story sir

No really I was holding it
Just a minute ago

We have not received your bus ticket

Do you ever make exceptions

No we don't sir

You know they have free pizza Wednesday

We don't serve pizza on the bus sir
We ask that you not eat on the bus
Did you find your ticket sir

I am still looking
I know it is here somewhere
What about free Tuesday

Tuesdays are not free sir
And today is Thursday

I found a coupon for a free ride

Sir
This coupon has expired years ago
And this is for the downtown bus
This bus goes everywhere
Except downtown

I remember now
The ticket is on my phone

Great sir
Can you show it to me

Well my battery is dead
Once on the bus
I can recharge it and show you

Nice try sir
Best one I've heard this week

Does the best of the week get a free ride

Sir
People are waiting to get on the bus
If you would step aside
Look for your ticket
When everyone has loaded
If you have your ticket
You can come on
If you don't
I am sorry
I can't give you a free ride

Well sir
Do you have a ticket

I have decided
It's such a nice day
I'll walk
It's only 60 blocks
In 103 degrees
Dragging my bum leg
On the hot concrete
With no water
My bad heart

Sir
just get on the bus

No
I have my dignity

Sir I need to leave now

Well if you insist

Are You Ready For A Change
(Performed with the band, Do It Now)

I woke up this morning
Everything seemed the same

Everything was different
Everything was different
A virus was in the air
Isolation lock down
Isolation lock down

Change Change Change
Are You Ready for a Change

I find myself feeling paralyzed
The endless misinformation
The endless lies and confusion
Elected officials talking & talking
About protecting us
The reality is they are neglecting us
The lies the mistrust
Is pulling us apart
We all need to pull together
We need to organize

Change Change Change
Are You Ready for a Change

People are in need
I am talking about my neighbors
I am talking about my friends
Those of us trying to get by
The money makers only see
Time to make money
Off the sick and dying
Selling needed supplies to highest bidders
Creating fear and scarcity
Raise those prices
Raise those prices

Change Change Change
Are You Ready for a Change

The bailout isn't for you & me
It's filling the bank accounts of the rich
Trillions magically appear
For those who don't need it
While those needing it most

Let them fight for crumbs
Let them fight for crumbs

Change Change Change
Are You Ready for a Change

Our Government
Refusing to acknowledge
Refusing to respond
The call for testing, needed supplies
Money to keep everyone afloat
Instead being told to ask nicely
Please don't let grandma, grandpa die

Change Change Change
Are You Ready for a Change

It's called genocide
If you can't murder by war
You murder with sanctions
Denying health care
Denying medical and food supplies
Demand regime change or die
Take no responsibility for using military might
Do what we say or die

Change Change Change
Are You Ready for a Change

Insanity over science
Who to believe

Conspiracies battle for my attention
While the news is used as propaganda
Who to believe
Is there a pandemic
Is there a grabbing of power
Was the system already crumbling
So why not crash it with a pandemic
The perfect excuse
The virus did it
Shut everything down
Put everyone out of business
The rich got richer
The virus did it
We are bankrupted
Lost many of our freedoms
The rich got richer

The rich did it

Change Change Change
Are You Ready for a Change

Our leaders, our governments
Tell us what a great job they are doing
The best job ever
So many lies yet many believe
When it's so obvious
The earth and all life
Is being destroyed
For the almighty dollar
"Believe me it's going to be the best dollar ever"

Change Change Change
Are You Ready for a Change

A cry for wanting our lives back
I wish things were normal again

We are never going back
To what was called normal
Nature and all life being expendable
We are never going back
To what was called normal
Now is the time
Now is the time

Change Change Change
We really need a change
We really need a change
Change Change Change

Billy Deserved It

When the camera
Focuses in
The audience sees
A poet at a microphone
Saying the next poem
Is about bullying

A guy yells
From the audience
You wimp

The poet recognizes the voice
Says is that you Billy

Billy yells back
Yeah
I should have drowned you
In the toilet at Deadend High School
When I had the chance

The poet says
Step into the light
So I can see if it is really you
Billy steps into the light
The poet says yeah
It is you
You still have the same smirk
And pulls out a gun
And shoots Billy several times

A waitress runs up
What is going on here
Looks down at the body

The poets say
I shot Billy
She says
Is that Billy

From Deadend High School
The poet says yeah
The waitress grabs the gun
And shoots Billy several times

The owner comes over
Sees the waitress with the gun
Takes it away
What is going on

She says I shot Billy
The owner says
That's Billy from Deadend High
Everyone nods
He shoots Billy several times

The police arrive
They ask who the victim was
On finding out
They shoot Bill several times

His body was then removed
No one was arrested

The poet didn't feel the need
To recite the poem on bullying
Instead he started to recite
How lonely they were
When the waitress
Started screaming
I loved you
You rejected my love
You want to be lonely

The poet
Deceides to read a different poem
Called
Dealing with your shit
In public

Clouds, Hopes, Dreams

When you open your eyes
What do you see

Are you in a war zone
Are you in the woods
Are you in a hospital ward
Are you seeing death and destruction
Are your seeing beauty

Yoko Ono said living in Japan after the bombings
Only wanted to look up into the sky
To watch the clouds
See how they changed
It gave her hope that things do change

You can dream
You see dragons
Faces
Wild horses
Whole stories unfold
Shown the unfamiliar
The abstract
Formations that don't fit
Into neatly defined boxes
The beauty that is shown and washed away
There is no holding on
Only taking in
Appreciating
Having to let go
The continual changes
The darkness
Then the dawn

The clouds passing over head
Here comes a story
Here comes a storm
Here comes relief from the sun

Look at the beauty
To be overwhelmed
Not to be taken for granted

Will never be the same
It is all there for us to see

Have you looked up
Do you see
Do you feel the hope
Do you dream

Here come the clouds

Here come the clouds

Don't Forget the Merch

Santa is White
Jesus is White

Some say there is a black female Santa
Along with a black female Jesus

And they are not happy
No ones seems to notice them
On social media
No one is liking their pages
They get hate mail
Why can't they just accept
The present narative

They don't understand the economics of it
What are we going to do with all the merch
We have with white Santas on it
Not to mention all the accessories for white Jesus
It would be an economic disaster

It's not environmentally the right thing to do
To fill our landfills with all that merch
Without selling it first

It doesn't matter that it's all a lie
A made up story
We have them believing
They are buying the merch

We need to transition slowly
What if we start with action figures
Of black worker elves
Standing around Santa
And slowly build towards
One of the elves working their way up
When Santa retires
We'll start with a lightly colored tan male
Change moves slowly

As far as the black female Jesus
We make up the story
A black female prostitute
That Jesus saves
A miracle
Yes that's it there's a miracle
The black female prostitute is turned into
A lightly colored tan male healer
Who carries on Jesus's work
When we retire Jesus in the future

After we sell all the merch

Listen
Change happens slowly
We need time
To dump all the merch

The Door

Prompt : The Poem,
"Prospective Immigrants Please Note"
by Adrienne Rich

One of my grandfathers
Told a story
About him being a child
Coming to this country
That a brother met him
At immigration
Told him
His name was Richmond
Kept repeating
Tell them you are a Richmond

His real name
Is never remembered
By his kids
The grandkids
Don't know it

Another story was
Everyone within a two block area
All changed their names
To the same name
From then on
Back room conversations
Before weddings were needed

When looking for work
If they heard your name
They would hang up the phone
If you gave them a name they liked
You could at least show up
Get your foot in the door

When they saw you
They knew you didn't match the name
At least you got your foot in the door
Sometimes it would be
Slammed

The ones who survived
Found ways
To get their foot
In the door

Family Traditions

I saw grandma
Run over the Tax Man
With the tractor
Everyone cheered
She still went to prison
I grew up with an attitude

Eveyone remembers
It as a miracle
The day I fell into the hay baler
After all the crunching sounds
Highlighted with my loud screams
I popped out the other end
In one piece

What I remember
Was being amazed
That my phone didn't get crushed
And that someone had pushed me in

When I was older
I was trying to
Make my living
As a Cowboy
I realize
Thing weren't going as I had planned
The morning
I had to eat my horse

On my death bed
The holyman who had been called
Said he wouldn't give me my last rights
I hadn't given his church any money
I started whispering
He leaned in close

Which made it easier for me
To shoot him at close range

With my last words

Here I come grandma

Firing Squad

I was asked
Did I want a blindfold
Did I want to say anything
Since I had one last request
Before the firing squad was given their orders
I said I did want to say something
To those who were going to kill me

As they all stood in a straight line
Guns raised pointing at me
I took my time to look each of them in the eye
One of them lowered his gun to his side

I started talking
I told them I wanted
To tell them a little about myself
I would skip over the night
My mother and father made love
I wouldn't bore them
With my cuteness as a baby
Those first few years
How even me hiding
Behind a door and shitting in my pants
My mother remembers fondly

I wouldn't bore them with my anxieties
Of my youth
Instead let me tell you how beautiful life is
The eating of good food,
I described one of my specialities
And maybe they would like me to make it for them
When I got to the dessert another of the men
Lowered his gun.

I talked philosophy and religion
How we are all one
Another of the men lowered his gun

I brought up my love for dogs and cats
I talked about my favorite dog, and one of my smartest cats
And another lowered his gun

I talked of family and being there for those who I loved
Who loved me
I asked if they wanted to see
Photos of my granddaughter
Another lowered his gun

There was still one who had his gun raised
Still pointing at me
Would he shoot
Even if he hadn't been given the order
Thinking he was saving the world from my kind

With him I knew I had to appeal to his soul
I said that I could make him a lot of money
I knew the secrete of how to make
Water into wine
With his help
We could have more money
Than either of us imagined possible
If I could
I would make us all some wine now
So we could celebrate

He had looked up from his gun
Still pointing it at me
I knew his soul needed more
I offered a 70 30 split
Giving him the 70 %

He lowered his gun

At that moment the captain
Who had been standing next to me
Took out his gun
His brother owns the local winery
And doesn't like competition

29

As he raised his gun to shoot me
The first fellow in the firing squad
Had raised his gun
And shot the captain
As he went to shoot me
The captain was pushed back
By the bullet hitting him
Having him raise his hand a bit
And instead of blowing off my head
He blew off one of my favorite hats

Years later I question my decision
To talk to the firing squad
As I am cooking endless meals for these guys
And I am always behind
In making of the wine

Grocery Bagger at 70

Applying at my local grocery store
To bag groceries at 70

On the application
I wrote down
I was
An artist / poet
I performed at
The Edinburgh Fringe Festival
Crisis-crossed the US
Featuring at festivals on the main stages
Traveled internationally
Performed
In Sweden, Hungary, Senegal....

At the interview
I was asked
Did I know not to put the eggs
On the bottom

Did I know that tomatoes can
Get crushed by can goods

Did I know that putting all cold items
Together helps keep them cold
And to not put them on top of peaches

Did I know to bag fish and meat
Their bacteria separate from the other foods

Did I know not to put the bread and bakery items
On the bottom

Finally could I manage only having
Two bathroom breaks
And no eating snacks

On a trial run
I was way over time
On bagging a mock up grocery sale
I was told not to spend time
Trying to arrange things artistically
That color coordination didn't matter

After a few days of training
I was ready for the front lines

Where I was told not to talk to the customers
They weren't interested
In hearing my poems

I was told not to tell people
Not to buy items
I thought were bad for them

It was not my business
If someone was
Only buying gallons of ice cream
Donuts and cases of diet soda

And especially not to mention
That items were cheaper
Down the block

I lasted long enough
To finally meet
Miss Jones
The day she chose
My register to check out
I had seen her
Walking her dog
Around the loop
At our assisted living complex

Here she was handing me her
Homemade cloth bag
Our eyes met
I knew this was fate bringing us together
Grateful for this opportunity to meet
As I put her groceries in her bag
I whispered
My recipes
For her tomatoes
Zucchini
And hot peppers
That was the last bag of groceries
I bagged
I was fired

That evening
We celebrated
With a scrumptious meal
While I read her my poetry
And she read me hers

Change Direction

Buffalo mid 1970's
I have a room with all windows
Overlooking the street
It was a porch that was made into a room
I can watch all kinds of scenes on the street

Today is a snow day
Not unusual for Buffalo
My car is snowed in
I am smoking a joint
Listening to music
Watching the snow coming down
I see an old woman
Walking up the street
Towards a bus stop
On the other side of the street
She has a big coat on
A babushka on her head
She is having a really hard time walking
The snow is deep
The wind is brutally cold

I wasn't going anywhere
Snow was piling up
I am smoking joints
Watching the snow fall
And this old lady
Standing waiting for a bus
Wondering were the buses even running

She is not standing still
She is bobbing up and down
As if the movement is keeping her warm
She is looking in the direction
Of where the bus would be coming
She steps out into the street
In the hopes to get a better look

She keeps doing this
As if it is a technique
To make the bus come sooner
Maybe if you at least
See the bus
It would give you the hope
It is on its way
The strength to hold on
As the wind howls
I can see by the look on her face
There is no bus coming

All of a sudden a bus pulls up
Across the street
Where there is another bus stop
Going the other way
She looks at it as it pulls away
The snow is blowing
She tries to cover her face
She is out in the street again
She is starting to resort to drastic measures
She starts to try to hitchhike
She doesn't put out her thumb
She is just eyeing the cars going by
If they look safe
Then she suddenly put up her thumb
But it is too late
They are already by her
She gets braver and braver
As she is getting colder and colder
Now she is just waving her hands
Looking crazy
Cars are now speeding by

Suddenly she is crossing the street
There is another bus going the other way
She stands there
When the bus stops and the door opens
She is talking to the bus driver
The bus driver is pointing

Saying he is going this direction
He's shrugging his shoulders
Must be telling her
He has to continue on
Suddenly she is getting on the bus
Pays her money
Sits in the front seat
Talking to the bust driver
The bus takes off in the opposite direction
This spoke to me about life
or maybe it was the pot

There are times you just need
To change direction

Flash Cards
(Performed with Do It Now

Flash cards
The height of technology
When I was growing up
It was a paper card
With a question
On one side
The answer was on the other
5 plus 5
9
No
12
No
35
No
Johnny you're guessing
it's 10
And they would show you the other side
There was the 10

It would be nice to have
Flash cards for Congress
What is environmental protections
Cutting trees
No
Fossil fuels
No
Corporate immunity
No

Some parents would practice
With their children
A caring mom
Who doesn't want you to fail
Gives you hints
The answers
Then they would wonder why
You are failing at school

At school is when these
Flash cards of devastation
Would inflect their trauma
The teacher would hold up
The card for Billy
The boy before you
His flash card was
9 multiplied by 4
36 Billy said proudly

I was next
I was ready
I had been
Looking up the answers on multiplications tables
And I had the answers written on my hand
The teacher turned to me
Held up the next card
What is 4,872,490
Divided by 5/16th

Happening once
You could say HA HA
Every freaking time
This is the kind of flash card you get
Every freaking time
No one seems to understand the trauma
All the therapists couldn't stop laughing
You start to ask yourself were you exaggerating
The humiliation, the failure
Feeling doomed
Cursed, singled out
When I try to explain
To my granddaughter
That I was asked
What is 4,872,490
Divided by 5/16th

They held up their phone
Smiling saying grandpa
It's 15,591,968

Did you forget to charge your phone grandpa?

I asked could they look up
Who invented Flash Cards?
Are they still alive?
Where do they live
She showed me two streets over
Maybe in the emotional state I was in
I shouldn't have gone over
I told the judge later
I just wanted to talk to them
How was I to know
They would open the door
Smile
And pull out a flash card
That asked
What is 6,500.042
Multiplied by 800.167422

I just want you to know
Having restrained meditation time
Heavy narcotics
And this ankle bracelet
That administers electric shocks
I have calmed down
And can almost see
It as the funnest thing
That could happen to anyone

To be honest
I still ask
Why me
Why
me

Merry Christmas 1970's

I was a performance Artist

It was December
During the Holidays
Christmas frenzy
I got this idea
I would dress up as
Santa Claus
I would build a large cross
I would glue fake money
To both of them
I wrote a poem
That started out
Ho Ho Ho HA

It had attitude
About commercialism
About the wars we were involved in
The homeless
Sexism
Racism
Violence
Everything I am still talking about today

I was in the student union
Of the University of Buffalo
Norton Hall
Where there were many tables
People handing out leaflets
I was greeting people in my Santa outfit
Carrying my cross and handing out my poem

One of the many groups there
Was a Christian group
An older man at the Christian table
Recruited 4 to 5 younger guys
Pointing me out
They came at me

They pushed me into
A dead-end hallway

Christian young men threatening me
Going to give me a good beating
Teach me a lesson
For defacing the cross – Jesus
Somehow before the pounding started
I asked them if what they were doing
Was very Jesus like
I continued my questioning
Asking them did they even know
Why I had money on the cross
Why I was dressed as Santa
Why I had the two of them together
Of course being an Artist
I wasn't quite sure why I was
Dressed up like this
It seemed like a good idea at the time

Back to the Christian thugs
I told them
That I too was upset
How Jesus was being sold
I managed to convince them
That we were both on the same side
We all thought Jesus said some cool stuff
I was released
The old guy was not happy
I continued to hand out my poem

The only other attack I encountered
Was from someone who came up to me
And asked when was I going to have an original idea
They informed me of an action that took place in Norway
Which I had no idea about
Many years later I saw a movie of that action

Hundreds of people dressed as Santas
Breaking into abandon factories

Giving it back to the workers
Along with many other actions
Including all of them walking into
The biggest department store in the city
Taking things off the shelves
And handing them to everyone
Saying the workers owned the goods they produced

Over the loud speaker the store manager
Is saying they are not the official Santas
Put the stuff back
The movie ends
With little kids screaming
As police officers
Are beating Santas

Once I ran out of poems
I decided to go home
I realized I needed some food
So I went shopping
Keeping on the Santa suit
But I ditched the cross

On my way to the market
As I walked along
I asked people I met
If they were good?
If I would have realized
What an amazing pick up
Outfit the Santa Clause suit was
I would have worn it more often

On asking if they were good
People would cuddle up
And say
Santa come to my place
And I'll show you

Others pulled out their wallets
And asked how much did I need
To disregard any negative info

At the super market
I asked the cashier
Did Santa have to pay
I said
The food was for the reindeer
I almost got out without paying

Once I got back to my rented room
Sitting next to the radiator
Trying to keep warm
Thinking about the people
Who wanted to take Santa home
Thinking about the Christian thugs
I wondered
Could art really change the world

I tried
Ho Ho Ho HA

The Time I Met Hunter Thompson

I met Hunter in a small town gas station
Hunter's Gas
I had broken down there
So I got to hang with him for a few days
He told me how everyone thought
He was Hunter S. Thompson the famous writer
Especially since he had up on his sign
Quotes by Hunter S. Thompson
Today's was

"Buy the ticket, take the ride."

Except this town wasn't on the bus route
So I was stuck there broken down
It felt like I had entered the Twilight Zone
Feeling like each day's new quote
Was a personal message to me

"When the going gets weird, the weird turn pro."

Hunter admitted he was cashing in
On people thinking he was Hunter S. Thompson
Selling them T shirts, coffee cups, taking pictures etc
He admitted it helped him sell a lot of gas
He hated being asked all the time
About drugs and alcohol
Did he have any to sell
When this was a dry county
The sign read

"I hate to advocate drugs,
alcohol,
violence,
or insanity to anyone,
but they've always worked for me."

Once the part arrived for my van
I had to find someone who could put it in

I had no tools with me
Hunter just sold gas
And Hunter S. Thompson paraphernalia
That day the sign read

"A man who procrastinates in his choosing
will inevitably have his choice made for him
by circumstance."

So I kicked into action
Hitching rides to find tools
Or someone who could help
I was going down blind alleys
That were dead ends
When I thought I had reached
My breaking point
The sign read

"The Edge…
there is no honest way to explain it
because the only people who really know where it is
are the ones who have gone over."

That day a woman showed up in a van
She had all kinds of tools
Could fix anything anywhere
And she started on my van
The sign read that day

"I have a theory
that the truth is never told
during the nine-to-five hours."

I learned a lot from her
We talked about everything
After one of our heated discussions
About our government
We looked up at the sign

"In a closed society
where everybody's guilty,
the only crime is getting caught.
In a world of thieves,
the only final sin is stupidity."

She had my van running better
Than when it was new
She wanted to take it for a test run
That day the sign read

"Faster, faster, faster,
until the thrill of speed
overcomes the fear of death."

I was glad to get back to Hunter's alive
I could hit the road again
I stood outside of Hunter's
After filling up my tank
And buying a coffee cup
You can always use a coffee cup
Watching the frenzy inside
People trying to get pictures with Hunter
Thinking he was Hunter S. Thompson
That day the sign read

"For every moment of triumph,
for every instance of beauty,
many souls must be trampled."

I left there thinking
Maybe I'll read some Hunter S. Thompson
I'll put it on the list

I Think He Could've Made It

I think he could've made it

If he would've just left the Heroin alone

Didn't drink hard liquor day and night

The cocaine didn't help

The pain killers by the handfuls
Didn't take the pain away

He was an amazing guitar play
Could he play

He was always pushing himself
Dropping 20 hits of acid at once
To see if he could handle it

Always testing himself and feeling like he failed

Some say he had a destructive streak
I think he could've made it

If he would've just wanted to live

In The Streets
(Performed with Do It Now)

The Sun was shining
The left and the right
Both were in the streets
Holding the same sign
Question Authority
Where is the truth

Some are screaming
Let me have my shit job back
For low wages
I have no money
Any money looks better then none

What is held in common
They both know the government is lying
The rich are getting richer
They don't give a rat's ass about us
One side blames the system
The other blames their neighbor
They see each other as the enemy

The rich get richer
The rich get richer

One side believes the lies
The others studies conspiracies
Where's the truth

The rich get richer
The rich get richer

One side goes to churches
Who take all their money
Molest their children
Spreading hate towards non-believers

The other side dances at a fire
Naked
Chanting
Seeing the demons outside and within
Can't seem to organize

The rich get richer
The rich get richer

How quickly it all happens
Everything is closed
All the money is gone
Local business crushed
The chain stores, chain restaurants, millionaires get bailouts
We wait for the crumbs

The rich get richer
The rich get richer

Where is the truth

The truth is obvious
The rich get richer
The rich get richer

We fight for the crumbs
Blame each other

The rich get richer
The rich get richer

It's Not Working
(Performed with Do It Now)

Hello Hello
Is anyone there
Can you hear me
Can you hear me

Do I have a live person on the line

Yes you do sir
I can hear you loud and clear
What can I do for you

Finally I get to talk to someone
Have you looked out the window lately
Have you looked out there
I don't think it's working
It's not working for me
I don't think it's working for a lot of people

What is actually the problem sir?

I am trying to tell you it's not working out there for us

When did you start feeling this sir

I think when I was offered that deal
When you could get
6 for 3
Or maybe when I could get
12 for 7
I am not sure
It always seemed like a deal
In the end I am in debt
I owe zillions of dollars
It's just not working
I mean come on
Do the math

I am not sure what you are complaining about Sir
This is what everyone does
This is the norm
Everything seems to be working just fine
In fact I can offer you a deal now
I can offer 20 for 10
We usually don't do that

I don't want your deals
Don't you understand

So you don't want to be very cooperative
Is that what it is
You should really learn how to cooperate
For then things would go a lot smoother
If you would just do what we wanted you to
It would be a lot easier for you you know

It's not my fault
I am tired of you guys trying to blame me
For everything you are doing
You know what you can do
You can tell those in charge
To go shove it

That's not very nice sir

I am tired
I have been on the phone
Trying to explain for over an hour

Sir you seem to exaggerate
We have only been on the phone
For 56 minutes and 40 seconds

That's it I've had it
You can go screw yourself
You know what
I am on a ledge right now
I am jumping because of you

What do you think of that
Here I go

Sorry to hear that sir
We will make sure we get out a card
To your family
We will send our regards
We will send our prays

Silence
Dial tone

Leaving Soon

I am broadcasting from
Leaving Soon Senior Home's
computer room

This might be my last communication
I am hoping my message gets out
Some doubt any will listen
I think it's worth a try

Each generation is faced with
Wars and environmental destruction
As a way of life
It doesn't have to be this way

When you are young
Everything takes forever
I can tell you that changes
Suddenly it all is happening faster
I am telling you life is short

It's important to take care of yourself
But even with a healthy life style
One day your body starts to not work
In the past you healed
You expected it to get better
You will have to face at some point
It doesn't heal, get better
The end is near

In case you think you have all the time in the world
I am just here to remind you
You run out of time
Live today
Live today

Over and out

Looking Out the Window

You never know what you will see
Looking out the window

Looking out the window
I see the sun shining on the snow

Looking out the window
It's hard to see anything
The rain is pouring down

Looking out the window
Watching big birds
Push little birds off the bird feeder
Watching a gang of little birds
Push the bigger bird off
The bird feeder looks low
They fly to the window
Looking in
I go out and fill the feeder
Now watching once again
The struggle to survive

Looking out the window
I am looking at a brick wall

Looking out the window
I am looking into your window
Does a relationship build
Never start
Do we agree we can watch
Do we wave
Are the curtains closed
To intimate moments

Looking out the window
Crowds of shouting people
Waving signs
Whose side are you on

This doesn't seem to be the time
To tell them they are stepping
On my dandelions

Looking out the window
There is a large explosion
I see nothing of what I saw before

Looking out the window
I am reminded
Of one of the chores on my list
Wash the windows
I had wanted to just sit on the couch
And look out the window

Looking out the window
See my love walking
Back towards the house
Waiting to hear the door open

Lost.........Released

"Get Out Of Here..."

Those are the words I will always remember
I heard them the day I left Buffalo, New York
The city of no illusions
In a VW Van, 1979
I was headed towards Western Massachusetts
Granola Valley
As it was called by a trucker

Everything I owned was in that van.
Much of it could have been left in a dumpster in Buffalo
Instead I was schlepping it to parts unknown
To a place I was told was filled with artists
Where I wanted to be

In those days it was either the radio or a cassette player
Providing the tunes
There was one rolled joint with the rest well hidden
For there had been too many times
For no reason other then being a long hair in a VW van
I would be pulled over and searched
They would be hoping to find
A bag of pot laying somewhere
Or like some very stoned friends
Who just had 2 pounds sitting in the back seat
While they rolled joints and cranked the tunes

I usually rationed myself to a joint or two
The rest for the party once I got to my destination
It's about 8 – 9 hours from Buffalo to Western MA,
Doing only 50 at top speed and with taking breaks

After the going away party
I hit the road
Somewhere around Syracuse
I smoked my joint and cranked up the tunes
Determined to make some time

Somewhere around Albany
I decided to stop at a rest area
Roll another joint
This time I got lazy
Which I always told myself
Not to do
Left the bag between the seats
After smoking the joint
I thought to myself I must be getting close
I had some vague memory that I was looking for RT 9
Suddenly there was an exit sign for RT 9
I took it
Happily thinking this driving would be over
Once I got on to RT 9 nothing looked familiar
I had been to the area
I drove for a bit and none of the names of the towns
Rang any bells.
Finally I saw that I could make a left and get off RT9
It was a quiet street with very big houses
I pulled over and parked
Turned down the music and got out the map
I wasn't anywhere near where I needed to be
I was just a little south of Albany
There was a Rt 9 there but not the one I needed
So it was back to the highway and keep driving

Except
There were sirens, screeching tires
Suddenly my car was blocked in by police cars
With police standing outside of my van
With guns pulled
Yelling for me to keep my hands up
Get out of the van slowly
Leaning against the van
Arms and legs stretched out
There were dogs in the police cars growling and barking
The police were yelling shut up
When I tried to find out what was going on
I thought I am screwed
In all this mayhem another unmarked car pulled up

A large Black man in a suit got out
Started giving orders sending the police who were there
To the house I was parked in front of

The dogs were released towards the house
I was suddenly standing there leaning against my van
With just this Black detective
I looked at him and said
I don't know what is going on
I stopped to look at my map
I am not from the area
I was lost, and obviously
I am in the wrong place at the wrong time
He looked at me in silence
Another police car pulled up,
Two police and more barking dogs
The policeman in the passager side of the car
Sticks his head out
Says to the detective
As he is looking at me and what I am wearing
Says the radio description of who they
Were looking for matches what I had on and looked like
As I looked at that policeman
He just stared at me and smiled
The detective told them to take the dogs to the house
They acted like they wanted to stay
Take me into custody
He said he would handle me
They went off, when they left he turned to me and said
This house you are parked in front of
Has just been robbed
The alarms went off
You pulled in
I figure you're the getaway car
I was trying to wrap my head around that
Out of all the places I would pick
To get lost and look at a map
Would be where a house was being robbed

I looked at the house, I looked back at him and I said,
Please take a look in to my van
Which was packed to the gills
I doubt very much that what you will see in it
Would have come from a place like this
And that there is no room
For me to take anything else
I pointed to the map on the dashboard
I thought this is my hope
He will see that it all matches my story
He told me to move away from the driver's door.
As he went to stick his head in
My hopes sank with remembering my laziness
Leaving the pot out somewhere
It seemed like a long moment
Watching his head turn this way and that   Looking
He then walked away from the van and stood off to the side
We could hear the dogs barking, he looked at me,
I looked at him, if he saw the pot he didn't bring it out
It was silent for what seemed a long time
We listen to the dogs and people yelling
He suddenly made a move and said

"Get out of here"
The way he said it was obvious no more talking,
No delaying, get in the van and get out,
I turned the key and said please start
The sound of the engine that I would soon be replacing
Sounded so good
As I pulled out, I said through the open window
Thank you,
He turned away as if to not see me leave
I drove off,
Looking in the rear view mirror
All the way to the highway…

I made it to Western MA

She Told Me
She Was the Devil's Mistress

My momma wanted me to marry
Betty Sue
But the Devil had other plans for me
Betty Sue was my childhood sweetheart
We use to hold hands
At Sunday school
She used to sit on the porch swing
With my momma
Sipping lemonade

I was always trying to get Betty Sue
To come into the barn with me
Momma had warned Betty Sue about the barn
"Why do you think that cat
Walks in alone
And comes out with kittens?"

One hot summer day
I went exploring
For a new swimming hole
I found one
But I wasn't alone
There was a beautiful naked woman
Stretched out on the rocks
She invited me to share her rock
She encouraged me to get naked
Telling me of the health benefits
Of swimming naked

Remembering my momma
Always telling me to take care of myself
Stay healthy

We jumped into the cool water
A few times
Soon after I was
Singing out to the lord

OH MY GOD

When I was leaving
I asked her
Her name
She just gave me a big smile

Momma wanted me to marry Betty Sue

Mommy Why
(Told to me by a student)

He said, he and his brother
Would be called by his mother
Into the room
Where she was sitting
She would say
She was going to commit suicide
She would tell them
Go and get me
A knife from the kitchen
So she could kill herself
They would cry and scream
Pleading with her to not kill herself
Refusing to go and get the knife
Then she would beat them
For not listening to her
And getting the knife

When he was a teenager
He walked around
With his long hair
Covering his face
One day he started calling
Chinese restaurants
Saying he had pictures
Of dead dogs and cats
They were using in their food
At first he asked for money
To buy a pizza
An older relative found out
Wanted in on the deal
Asked for hundreds of dollars
The police found them
They were arrested
He went to jail
Experiecned more violence

He asked me why was I so nice to him

My New Year's Resolution 2021

For future generations
I will remind myself and everyone
The power
of strikes
resistance
creativity
organizing
for change

Darling
Would you like to hear my New Year's Resolution?
It starts with coffee, obviously
Lots of it
And of course a cream puff

I'll get you two cream puffs and a thermos of coffee
So you will have the energy
To dedicate each day to organizing strikes
Developing new forms of creative resistance
Yes the lying, cheating scumbags
Will be going to prison
If you see me falter in my attempts
To keep my New Year's Resolution
I will be looking to you for help

Happy New Year

Patron Saint of Lost Causes

I woke up thinking
I needed to pray
To the patron saint of lost causes

Everyone prays in their own way
I hadn't really paid attention
During catechism
So I wasn't sure how to reach
The patron saint of lost causes
Scenes of praying and candles
Are always in the movies
I wondered
How many candles
Do I need
To let the
Patron saint of lost causes
Know I was needing their help
I filled the room with all the candles
I had

Wondering what the next step was
I remembered there was something
Said about wine
So I started drinking
As I sat there
Looking at all the candles flickering
The wine was gone
I was thinking maybe
The patron saint of lost causes
Was hearing my call for help

When the cat came in
Knocked over a number of candles
The curtains caught fire
I managed to run out
With the cat
As I watch the place burn down

As I watched it burn
I thought
This
Is really the time
You need
The patron saint of lost causes

Then the police showed up
Of course after hearing my story
I was arrested
Thrown in jail
As I sat in the cell
I thought
This is when I need the
patron saint of lost causes

You get the idea
As things kept happening
I kept thinking
This is the time to call
The patron saint of lost causes

At some point
I realized it was time to call
The patron saint of
Get your shit together

Pissing in the Front Yard

He was born in a shack
In the woods
As he grew up
Trees were cut down
The trail near the shack
Turned into a dirt road
As a kid
He would run outside to take a piss
He like to piss in what became known
As the front yard
He liked the big trees
On that side of the house
While pissing he would
Look at them
Wondered what it would be like
To climb them
As he grew older
The dirt road became gravel
Cars would pass by now and then
He had climbed the trees
He felt at home pissing by the big trees
That were still there
As time went on
The road became paved
More trees had been cut down
Cars passed more often
More houses could be seen
There were lawns
His place stood out
Things grew wild
He didn't have a lawn

He became known
As the crazy old guy
He was in his 90's
When he was arrested
For pissing in his front yard
He stunk up the back of the police car

His piss stained pants
He was asked why
Wasn't he taking care
Of himself
He said he couldn't
And there was no one
Who was helping him

The old man
Asked why couldn't he
Just keep living where he was
Die in the front yard
Trying to take a piss

The old man asked in court
Is there a law
Against pissing in the front yard
A recess was called

As the court secretary searched for the law
Someone known as a social worker
Was looking for services that could help
Clean up the place, getting food delivered
Taking care of him
The judge knew
The system wasn't working
There were long lines
Trying to place people
As it is called in the trade

The judge knew he had
A case coming up
With a group of youths
Who lived in the old man's neighborhood
Had gotten arrested for being teenagers
He decided he would sentence the boys
To planting large bushes
In the old man's front yard
So he could continue to piss
With the big trees

An agency was found
Who said they would go out and help

The teenagers got to know the old guy
Found he was pretty funny
They got jobs bringing in his wood

He continued to piss in his front yard
Laughing out loud
As he watched the teens climb the trees

Who Works for Who
(Performed with Do It Now)

Unidentified

Unidentified

Federal agents

Federal agents

Operating
Without accountability
How do we stop them
Who will tell them
They can't kidnap people
Off the streets
Where are the police
Why aren't the police stopping
These kidnappings

Who works for who
Who works for who

The people are in the street
They want a change
Stop the violence
The racism
The hording of wealth
Stealing from the poor
Stop raping the earth
Everyone on it

2020
Police brutality
Police violence
Cvil rights violations
Excessive force
Beatings
A cry for justice

Brings more
Vicious beatings

Early records
suggest labor strikes
were the first large-scale incidents
of police brutality in the United States,
including events like
the Great Railroad Strike of 1877,
the Pullman Strike of 1894,
the Lawrence Textile Strike of 1912,
the Ludlow Massacre of 1914,
the Great Steel Strike of 1919,
And on and on and on
Paid thugs attacking the strikers
Why isn't the military stopping them
Protecting the people

Who works for who
Who works for who

Forcing so many into poverty
Desperate people are easier to control

Or are they
Or are they

Every camper knows
Don't get in between
A mother bear and her cub
Yes the moms came out
The dads
The youth where carrying the torch

The Bill of Rights, First Amendment
Freedom of speech, Freedom of assembly
Congress didn't get the job done
They left on vacation
When millions have no money or work
Today, people need food today

You don't go on vacation for a month
The virus has shut it all down
We need to keep it shut down
We are in the streets
Until real change happens

Who works for who
Who works for who

Wrong Person

You know
If you weren't such a thief
A no good lying so and so
Irresponsible
Careless heart crusher
Two bit lover
Never show Casanova
Burning down the house
Shit hitting the fan movie
I could almost fall for someone like you

You have to ask yourself why
What is the attraction
To jumping off the cliff
Did I at least bring water to stay hydraded

Those lies you called love
Those gifts bought with stolen goods
Your three sisters from different mothers
Two having your kids
The third tried to kill you
You told me she didn't understand you
There were so many other's lives destroyed
That you said was their fault
Like a moth to the flame
I could almost fall for someone like you

You have to ask yourself
Why
What is the attraction
To jumping off the cliff
I started to look over the edge
With the illusion
That I know what I am getting myself into

When you said you went to college
When really you were in prison
Yes I know you can learn a lot there

You did become a better safe cracker
You said you didn't what to be anyone's bitch
You wanted all of us to be yours

I could almost fall for someone like you
But I have asked myself
Why

I wear a parachute now
In case I stumble
My vision is better now
I can see the red flags flying
I know what not to get myself into

You're A White Man

In the early 70's
For a short time
Long hairs were called the new Niggers
This was before the police grew their hair long
Pulling their badges when you passed a joint
Hippies, Long Hairs
Were easily identified among the buzz cuts
You were chased out of stores
Businesses wouldn't serve you
The police pulled you over constantly
Searching for pot
A hippie always carries pot
If not the police plant some on you
So the newspapers can say
We got one of those dirty hippies
We are doing our job of cracking down on the disease

There was fear as more people started to grow their hair
Let it do its own thing, became a thing
There was a fear it's going to spread
It must be crushed

As hippies we moved to old neighborhoods
For the cheap rents and to be able to live in groups
Neighborhoods our parents left
As they moved up the ladder
Now the old neighborhoods were Black
We were told that is where the crime is
The areas of abandoned buildings
Absentee landlords
Those in the suburbs
Asked over and over
Why do they want to live like this
Many didn't have a choice

Hippies weren't trusted
Since they were downsizing
The have nots

Wanted what the hippes were giving up

Living in the Black area of Buffalo
I experienced
The Black Panthers
They came to town to help organize
Set up meetings for the neighborhoods
To discuss what was going down
To be prepared to fight
From house to house
Entering the building where the gathering was held
Everyone was searched
Especially myself being white
I was one of the few whites at the meeting

After the meeting
One of the Panthers brothers
Came over
Asked me questions
Why was I there
What was I doing in my daily life
I told him about my different projects / work
At the time I was going into Attica prison
Once a week following up on the demands of the prisonors
Who a few months earlier had a rebellion
Took over the prison
Demanding to be treated as human beings
The rebellion took place
Two weeks after the killing of George Jackson
at San Quentin State prison
Most of the 28 demands were agreed to
Yet in the end Governor Rockefeller
Ordered a massacre
Killing guards and prisoners

I went in once a week
To honor those who had died
By making sure the demands that had been won
Agreed to during the rebellion
Were actually being fulfilled

The conversation between us jumped topics
We talked of genocide in VietNam
Demonstrating against the military complex
Killings at Kent state
Helping the broken soldiers coming back from the war
The many assassinations
Fighting the environmental destruction
The greed and the lack of justice

I'll always remember the conversation
Especially how it ended
He thanked me for coming
The work I was doing
Then added
You know we can never trust you
I didn't respond
He asked me did I want to know why
I nodded
He asked me to hold up my arm
He put his next to mine
He said the reason we can never trust you
Is you can cut your hair
Shut your mouth
And blend in
He looked down at his arm
I can't hide that color
I have nowhere to hide
We can't trust you
When push comes to shove
Who are they going to shoot first
You can slide back in

I have nowhere to hide

Now 2020
Over 50 years
Massive demonstrations against the Gulf Wars
Black Lives Matter
The Occupy Movement
The Native Americans at Standing Rock
Wars continue as a way of life
Environmental destruction
Children in cages
There is a larger gap between rich and poor
The courts still favor the rich
Prison have become privatized
Run on their own rules
Creating prisoners is a business
The police have become more militarized
Unarmed citizens being killed

We need new tactics
To continue to organize for change

I was almost beat up
By punks at a Clash concert
Who were screaming at me
That hippies were dead

We are told the dream has died
Has it
It takes each of us to keep it alive
Even if all our hair has fallen out

Grandpa was a Sonofabitch

They say you can't take it with you
When you die
Some created pyramids
Filling rooms with all their toys
and servants
Grandpa planned his whole funeral
He ordered a special beer for the occasion
That was poisoned with crocodile bile
Grandpa had said he didn't like going first
Or anywhere alone
56 died from drinking that beer
Later it was found out
Grandpa hadn't died
He had arranged for a closed casket
He knew they would all be partying
Glad that he was dead
Now that they had gone first
He had a big smile on his face
As he drank the beer
In anticipation of seeing their faces

I Hate This Place

"Why am I here
Why must I suffer here
What is the purpose of my suffering"
"I tried to kill myself
And It didn't work
I want to leave now
I am done"

The father dies
His daughter
Went in and took off his watch
Put another one on
Thinking no one would notice
The gold watch
Replaced with a kid's watch

The brothers had gone in
Taken all of his tools
They weren't smart enough
To steal his watch
By putting on another watch

The mother and the other son noticed
As the vultures
Who hadn't been around for years
Tried to take
Expected everything

"My hopes and dreams drowned
In their actions
Their empty words and promises
Why am I here
Why must I suffer here
What is the purpose of my suffering
I tried to kill myself
And It didn't work
I don't know why I am here"

What Do You Do For A Living

At a party our main character was asked
What do you do for a living
I Kill
There was little reaction
Since everyone in the room kills
They were asking what do you kill
Do you kill small animals,
Mice, rats, the ones people hate
Or do you beat baby seals
Do you run a factory
Where you grind up lives for a profit
Making things no one really needs
Are you one of those
Who goes into nature
And rapes it
Shits all over it
Burns, chops it up
Turning earth's champagne
Water
Into a poison
That kills everything

The guests waited
Patiently to hear
What kind of killer he was
The silence was killing them
They lived on small talk at parties
So more questions
Did he kill with his barehands
Knives, guns
Sitting in a room
With a computer
Flying drones and killing people

Do you kill for your own food
Go hunting, fishing
Or you let others do the killing for you

Do you work in offices
Where endless questions
Are asked
Endless forms to fill out
Misleading questions
Complicating obvious answers
Creating incorrectly filled out forms
Rejected applications
Making you dead in the water
Are you the guy who hands out that paperwork

Don't tell us your are a two bit manager
Making others feel
Like they are losers
Destroying the willingness to live
Telling others they belong on the bottom

Our main charater told the guest
It was more hideous
Than anything they had mentioned
Or could be imagined
He wasn't sure they had the stomachs
For his type of killing

He asked
Is it easier to accept
The killing of others
As they are evil
Do you accept the killing of oneself
Wanting the pain to end
And is the killing of yourself
Quickly
Not as hideous
As killing yourself over years
Drinking yourself to death
Overdosing
Endless sabotaging yourself
Slowly killing any love that exists

He said his killing
Even made him sick
Just as he was going to tell them
They were interrupted
By the host of the party
Who was always coming up
With group party games to play
And was passing out funny hats
Trying to explain the rules
Many excused themselves
Saying they needed to
Powder their nose

Our main character
Had learned picking up dishes
Any party trash
Looks like you are helping
It gives you an acceptable excuse to leave
Assuming you would be back
While in the kitchen
Our main character meets
A kindred spirt
Who had collected glasses
They both laughed
They lingered
Then they asked
What do you do for a living

Amazed
(Performed with Do It Now)

Are you amazed
At what is going on
After all of the lies

I find myself dispassionate
Hoping for the truth
I stay unemotional as the lies continue
You may mistake
My not being amazed
As if I am unconcerned
Yes I am jaded After 60 years
Of the lies
Of hatred
Of violence
The killing, In the endless wars
The indifference to life

I have become bored with the promises
I am not surprised when nothing changes
I may look unruffled as I am destroyed inside
Disinterest in working with habitual abusers
Flabbergasted bewildered and stunned
I am dumbfounded with the choices offered
I admit I was blindsided when I realized
We have to create the choices we need

We have to create
The choices we need
We need
To create the choices
We need

The School for the Protection of the Arts

Orwell warned us
How language would be used to control
Which words are put together
To create the opposite meaning
The use of the words to draw you in
Believing
Are your eyes open
What are your ears hearing
Do you trust your gut
Do you feel
The creativity
Or do you smell death

The arts are not being protected
They are being slowly killed
Not allowing for time to play
Create
Given paints, instruments,
Pen and paper
The belief that you have something to say

It seems so sinister
Can it be true
The School for
Protection of the Arts
Is really killing the arts
Killing creativity
Teaching painting by numbers
Being mechanical
Memorizing rules
Handing out the acceptable pieces
To be put together
To be called art
Anyone who tries anything
Different will be seen
As inferior
Their art will not be accepted

Not shown in galleries
Not supported
Hoping they will all go away

Throughout history
Many went there own way
Many straved while alive
Hailed as genius after they died

The school for protection of the arts
Is taking applications
You need not apply

The King of the Killers

Also know as
The Twofold Bay Killers
A true story

Between 1840 and 1930
A pod of Orca killer whales
Would assist whalers in hunting Baleen whales
One of the male Orca whales
Was named Old Tom
The whalers thought
Due to Old Tom's size
He was the leader
The King of the Orcas

The reality is Orca killer whales
Are led by a female

Old Tom had been given the job
To communicate
Negotiate with the Davidsons
Who were whalers
When the Orcas had worked together
To corner Baleen whales in Twofold Bay
Old Tom would then go to
The mouth of the Kiah River
Where the Davidson family had their tiny cottages
He would breach the water
He would tail slap over and over
Until the Davidsons responded
They would then go over together
And kill the Baleen whales

In all deals
If everyone gets what they what
Everyone stays happy
The Orcas wanted the tongue and the lips
Of the Baleen whales

The Orcas considered them delicacies
The Davidson whalers wanted
The profitable blubber and whalebone
The agreement was
The whalers would anchor the carcass overnight
While the killer whales ate only the tongue and lips
The Davidsons would come back
To harvest
The profitable blubber and whalebone
How this deal was first arranged
Is unknown
It went on for almost 80 years
The arrangement was called
"The law of the tongue"

Around the mid 1920s
A retired veterinarian, John Logan
His daughter Margaret
And third-generation whaler George Davidson
Were aboard Logan's motorized yacht
Logan had been out whale chasing
Old Tom showed up
And saw an opportunity
Old Tom forced a smaller Baleen whale
To the surface
Davidson's crew harpooned it
Davidson a third generation whaler
Had leaned
"The law of the tongue"
From his father and grandfather
Honoring the deal
He started anchoring the carcass
Logan saw a storm was coming in
"I don't want to lose this whale to the storm
Forget about Old Tom"

Logan then attempted to bring the carcass ashore
Not honoring
The law of the tongue
Davidson pleaded with Logan

Old Tom seeing what was going down
Decided he would take the carcass for himself
He grabbed on to the tow rope
And began to pull
A tug-of-war
Began
The yacht strained
Against Old Tom's might
Davidson pleaded with Logan
To stop
Logan gave his yacht full throttle
As they broke loose
They realized they had
Pulled out many of Old Tom's teeth
As a veterinarian Logan knew
It would be the death of Old Tom
Logan said "Oh God, what have I done?"

Old Tom's corpse washed ashore
Months later
His mouth had abscesses from missing teeth
He may have died of starvation
Old Tom's death was reported
In the Sydney Morning Herald
On September 18, 1930
The headline
"King of the Killers" has died
After Old Tom death
The Orca killer whales disappeared
There are many theories why

What was clear
Orcas and whalers
No longer worked together

Culture

People say they have a culture
I don't have a culture
My culture was lost
At immigration
Where names were changed
Where language's were discontinued
Where Polish and Prussian and Russian
Were not discussed
Where being Catholic or Jewish
Defined your team
What to do if you were both
Whose team are you on

Grandma had a strange smell
Made weird sounds
We didn't understand
She grabbed us in her strong arms
And squeezed us tight
Put coins in our little hands
There was nothing before being here now
There is no history to learn from
Try to not act Polish
Don't act Russian
We don't know wher Prussian is

Loose that accent
Loose that accent

Their lanaguge was structured differently
Jokes were made of how polacks talked
"Throwing the baby out with the bath water"
Throwing the horse over the fence some hay"
The polacks are stupid

Your are not your past
You are not your past

New arrivals to the neighborhood
Were told on arriving
Stop wearing those colorful clothes
That screams out you are polish
Look American
Buy your clothes at JC Pennies
Look like the people in
Look and Life magazines
Look American

I joined
Hippie counter culture
I wore the outfit to play the part
We were told you'er not allowed to create youe own culture
As with the Polish jokes
The counter culture soon had it's own sterotypes
Long hair, barefoot, dirty, sex crazy,
stoned, doesn't want to work
We asked what was wrong with that

Today our sense of identity is being trapped
In our choices about our sexuality
LGBTQIA
If you ask me
I try to keep Tuesdays open

Identities are created by which foods you eat
Do you have a social media following
Who likes you
Why doesn't Betty Lou give me any hearts

I have no grounding in any culture
Am told I am appropriating other cultures
So I belong to no one
I know very little about being Polish/ Russian
I only heard about my relatives in Poland
Throwing rocks at tanks
When we saw the pictures
In National Geographic

Everyone made jokes, laughed
Why would you throw rocks at tanks
They had nothing else to fight with
They weren't going down
They weren't going down wihtout a fight

I am told that my ancestors
Fought and killed each other
Over many generations
Hated each other
Tried to exterminate each other
As my mother and father representing all of this
Were brought together
In one of the factories
Where we were all Americans
Where we have been melted together
Where we have lost all traces of where we originated
Where I wander lost
In the grave yard of buried cultures
I wander lost

Bug Splat

In a report
It stated
Drone strikes 380
Estimated
3,500 dead
200 children dead

From where a drone operator is sittting
Looking at a screen
The target being shot
Is one blurry blob of pixels

In the past
When there were a lot more bugs
When you drove at night
Your windshield would be covered
White splatters from the bugs
Hence the term "Bug Splat"

"Bug Splat" worked it's way
Into modern military slang
As a way of referring to a kill
"Bug Splat"
The name of the software
Used to operate the drones

Artists in Pakistan
With only their art as their weapons
Set up a giant installation
In the hopes to reach the drone operators

The "Bug Splat"
Are children
Mothers
Fathers
Lovers
Best friends

Language is used
To try and hide the violence
Atrocities being done

Recent examples
"Extraordinary Renditions"
"the seizure and transfer of a person to another country
for imprisonment and interrogation **if** suspected
of involvement with a terrorist group
without legal process"

Kidnapping

"Enhanced Interrogation"
Is a euphemism for the program of systematic torture of detainees

Water Boarding

It is so much easier to say and hear
"enhanced interrogation"
Not that you are drowning someone
So that they will say what you want

Everything is given a name
One type of missile is called Hellfire
Individual missiles have names
Predators
Reapers
From a quote describing the missiles
The names evokes
"the punishment in the afterlife adding to a sense of righteousness."

The terrorists are given names
Political terrorist
Social revolutionary terrorism
Nationalist-separatist terrorism
Religious extremist fundamentalist terrorism
Right-wing terrorism
Left-wing terrorism
Criminal terrorism

Pathological terrorism
Cross border terrorism
Domestic and international terrorism
On and on

It's easy to believe
There are a lot of terrorists

The UN Security Council Resolution 1566(2004) definition:
Criminal acts against civilians
Committed with the intent to cause death
Taking of hostages
To provoke a state of terror
Intimidate a population
To compel a government or international organization
To do or to abstain from doing
Any actions
Not approved by the terrorists

On the list of terrorist countries
The United States and Israel
Are not listed
Why

Why is a kid
Sitting in a room
Playing "Bug Splat"
With people more than 6,500 miles away

They have been called terrorists

It's not a game
Human beings are killing each other
Have been doing it
For Humdreds of Thousands of years
Those with the most
sopisticated weapons
And strategies
Dominate

Yes there is a cost
The Pentagon estimates cost
Of one new nuclear missile
At $95.8 Billion
That money could
House the homeless
Feed the poor
Provide health care
Improve, repair the infrastructure

The word Socialism
Is brought up
Which we are told is bad
Adding another Bug Splat
To the screen

Who Are You

Who are you
A simple question
You can answer it many ways
You could give your name
Some award you won

You didn't know
That when you walked
Into the room
Everyone in the room
Doesn't know who you are either
You can't blame them
Since you don't know who you are
How would they know
Who you really are

You've had this idea
That you were following a calling
To create who you
Think you are
Then you graded yourself on
Did you create the persona
That you thought was the real you

Then one day
You were sitting in a restaurant
When the little girl sitting
At the table next to yours
Turned
Looked you straight in the eyes
And says
You don't know who you are do you
Paused
You are never going to find out probably
Then turned back to her mother
Who was trying to explain
The universe

You were stunned
Left speechless
And suddenly it all felt meaningless
All the work creating this persona
Was it for nothing

When the waiter
Brought the check
It all became clear
You have done a good job
At selling your persona
You could pay the bill
And even leave a tip

National BeatPoetry Foundation Inc. awarded Paul Richmond

Massachusetts Beat Poet Laureate
2017 to 2019

U S National Beat Poet Laureate
2019 - 2020.

New Generation Beat Poet Laureate
2022 - Lifetime

Paul is best described as "political, deadpan and wryly humorous delivered in his own style". He has been called, "Assassin of Apathy – power of words / humor - on the unthinkable, the unsolvable, to analyze, to digest, to give birth to creativity and hope."

He has performed nationally and internationally

He created the project "Do It Now" working with different musicians, the core being Tony Vacca & John Sheldon who performed 12 shows as Do It Now at Edinburgh Fringe Festival Scotland 2018

He is also the publisher at Human Error Publishing, with over 50 writers in the catelog. Human Error Publishing produces monthly and yearly Word festivals and events.

More info: www.humanerrorpublishing.com

Other Books by Paul Richmond

No Guarantee's Adjust & Continue - 2007
Ready Or Not ....Living in the Break Down Lane - 2009
*Too Much of a Good Thing - In the Land of Scarcity
-Breeds Contempt* -2011
You Might Need a Bigger Hammer - 2015
Words 4 Sandwiches - 2017
The 24 Hour Store was Closed - 2020

Paul Richmond won the Miller Audio Prize in the humor category for "Life Stories." "Your piece blends the observational humor of stand-up comedy, the quick tempos and wandering melodies of jazz, and the clever linguistic turns of spoken word poetry. That is so deeply human, pointing out the joys and absurdities of living in our current moment."
  - Ann Elise Hatjakes Contest Editor, the Missouri Review

"Deadpan empathic rebellion" Like Paul himself, his poems take a poke at safe conventions and assumptions, conceptualization and monetization. He put together a jazz-word fusion band and took it international, forging bonds with empathic creative rebels in Scotland, Sweden, Hungary and Senegal. But he has also rambled through the poetry dens of Austin, my old home town. He's the outside voice befriending other outside voices."
Richard W. Horton

"Funtimes - I laughed out loud numerous times and when's the last time poetry did that for me? An engaging ride till the bitter end. I recommend this book for anyone looking to cool their jets. Inspiring and singular. Way to go, read it up!"
Amazon Customer

"Love the humor! Great understated delivery.....
your inflections and reflections say it all."
Denise Baxter Yoder

"I laughed, I teared, I felt the rage, all wrapped up
in perfectly executed phrases that only Paul could construct.
A treasure to read then read again. Hold up the mirror, look through the windows, pay attention then bang down that closed door...with bells on."   Louis

"No matter what topic Paul writes about his deftly applied skewers hit the heart of the matter dead on, even when approaching from an angle. There's a reason he's beat poet laureate. Recommended reading for all generations."
Amazon Customer

www.ingramcontent.com/pod-product-compliance
Lightning Source LLC
Chambersburg PA
CBHW071156090426
42736CB00012B/2350